Ketogenic Fat Bombs

Delicious Bites to Boost Your Energy

by
Sophia Rose

Table of Contents

Introduction

Congratulations on downloading your personal copy of *Ketogenic Fat Bombs*. Thank you for doing so.

The following chapters will provide you with over 101 delicious fat bomb recipes that will help you with your ketogenic lifestyle.

As you may or may not already know if you are on this diet, fat bombs are designed to be high in fat but low in sugars, proteins and carbohydrates. Whilst training this will allow your body to target the use of your fat supply as a main source of energy rather than using the carbohydrates as the primary energy source. Which in turn eliminates the fat off of those stubborn parts of your body (such as your core).

You will love learning these fabulous new fat bomb recipes, thanks again for choosing this one! Every effort was made to ensure it is full of as much useful information as possible. Please enjoy!

Remember with any foods or lifestyle diet the key is moderation! Only bake these for yourself once or twice a week to maintain/improve your body, we all love food but looking sexy has its rewards.

Congratulations on downloading your personal copy of *Ketogenic Fat Bombs*.

A Ketogenic Diet

The keto diet isn't something new. Dr. Russell Wilder from the Mayo Clinic came up with it in 1924. It was very effective for treating epilepsy. Once medication was invented in the 40s for seizures, it stopped being used as much. The research found that avoiding consuming food for a while, including carbs reduced how many seizures that a patient had.

This diet is low carb and is high in fat. The body won't require as many carbs and will start to burn ketones that it uses for energy. The body naturally reaches ketosis every day. It doesn't matter what you eat. Eating foods low in carbs will speed up this process. This is a completely safe and normal chemical process.

The body breaks down large amounts of protein and carbs into glucose. Glucose helps to create ATP. This is a fuel we need for our everyday activities and to maintain our bodies.

Ketosis happens when the body no longer has as much glucose or glycogen.

When your body doesn't have any access to food, such as when you are on a ketogenic diet or sleeping, the body will burn fats and creates ketones.

The body only needs a small amount of glucose to stay healthy. The body doesn't need carbs. The liver does its job by making sure your body has the glucose it needs.

Protein can also be changed into glucose, so make sure you don't eat too much or it can stop ketosis.

Ketosis will change the metabolism and turn you into a fat burning machine. When you first start the keto diet, changes will happen, and you may end up with the keto flu.

The keto flu can consist of, having bad breath, being moody, weakness while working out, having problems sleeping, and feeling tired. This won't happen to everybody and will go away after a week. It's just the initial shock of reducing you're carb intake. Extra water and salt can also help.

While calorie counting isn't necessary, as long as you keep carb intake low and protein moderate, you can still use ratios to count calories if you want. You will need 70% of your calories coming from fat, 20% should come from protein, and less than 10% should come from carbohydrates. The actual amounts will depend on your what your current size and weight is.

You can speed up ketosis by intermittent fasting. This means that for 16 to 20 hours a day, you don't eat. You make sure to consume your food within eight to four hours each day. This could mean you eat between 2 PM and 9 PM and fast from 9 PM to 2 PM.

You've probably heard of fat bombs. These treats are made up of mostly healthy fats. These could be eaten for a quick breakfast, pre- or post-workout or afternoon snack for someone doing a low carb diet because they won't disrupt ketosis. Which is great because that means you can have healthy sweets that won't hurt your diet.

These are little bites that are hard to eat too many because of the fat content. They are often shaped like balls or are made in muffin liners.

Most fat bombs will be sweetened with Stevia, which is a low-calorie sweetener. You can also use whatever low-calorie sweetener that you desire.

Recipe KEY:

- C= Cup
- Tsp= Tea spoon (The little spoon you use for your tea or coffee)
- Tbsp= Table spoon (The standard sized spoon that you eat your food with)
- Oz= Ounce (1 oz = 28.35 grams)

Brownie Fudge

Ingredients:

- ¾ cup coconut butter, melted
- ¼ tsp baking soda
- 2 tbsp coconut oil, melted
- 1/3 cup coconut milk cream
- 5 tbsp cacao powder
- ½ tsp vanilla bean powder
- ¼ tsp sea salt
- 1 egg
- ¾-1 cup sweetener
- 2 tsp vanilla extract

Instructions:

Combine the cacao, sweetener, salt, baking soda, and vanilla bean powder in one bowl. Beat the coconut butter, coconut milk cream, and coconut oil together in a separate bowl.

Mix in the egg and the vanilla to the wet bowl, then stir the wet and the dry ingredients together gradually. Make sure that there are no lumps.

Grease up a square baking dish and pour in the mixture. You should have your oven at 250. Place the brownies in for 20 to 25 minutes.

The center may seem to be uncooked, but it's fine as long as the edges are browned. Once the pan is cooled off, slide the brownies in the fridge. They should stay stored in the fridge and they are ready to eat after 3 hours in the fridge.

Lemon Fat Bomb

Ingredients:

- 7.1-oz coconut butter, softened
- Pinch salt
- ¼ cup coconut oil, softened
- 15-20 drops Stevia extract
- 1-2 lemons, zested

Instructions:

Allow the coconut butter and oil to come to room temperature. Once room temp, place everything in a bowl and mix together well, making sure the Stevia and zest are well distributed.

Grab silicon molds and fill with a tablespoon of the mixture and refrigerate until hard, about 30-60 minutes. Take out of the mold, to serve and keep in the fridge.

Ginger Fat Bomb

Ingredients:

- 2.6-oz coconut butter, softened
- 1 tsp ground ginger
- 2.6-oz coconut oil, softened
- 1 tsp sweetener
- 1-oz shredded coconut, unsweetened

Instructions:

Place everything into a large mason jar and screw on the lid. Shake it until all the ingredients come together.

Place the mixture in molds or an ice tray and place in the fridge until hard. Take out to serve and keep refrigerated.

Choco Walnut Bark

Ingredients:

- 1 tbsp heavy whipping cream
- 1 tbsp powdered sweetener
- 2 tbsp coconut oil, melted
- Dash salt
- 1 tbsp walnut halves, toasted

Instructions:

Mix the cocoa powder, salt, sweetener, and walnuts into the coconut oil. Beat in the heavy cream until it is all well mixed and creamy.

Spread this in a tray on the wax paper to a quarter inch thickness. Once it has cooled and hardened, break into pieces and enjoy indulging in this delicious fat bomb.

Maple Nut Fudge

Ingredients:

- 1 cup butter
- 1 tsp Stevia
- 8-oz cream cheese
- ¼ tsp ginger, ground
- ¼ cup Swerve
- 1 cup pecans
- 1 tsp maple extract

Instructions:

Melt the butter in a pot and allow it to brown. Stir in the sweetener and let it cook until it begins bubbling. Pour this into a bowl and stir in the extract and cream cheese.

Use an electric mixer until it comes together. Let it cool a bit, and then whip again. Separation is normal.

Mix in the nuts and ginger. Place parchment in a square baking dish and pour the mixture and refrigerate until hard. After it's hard, take it out and slice into squares to serve.

Peanut Butter Fudge

Ingredients:

- ¼ tsp sea salt
- 6 tbsp butter, softened
- ½ tsp vanilla
- 1 cup peanut butter
- ¾-1 cup powdered sweetener
- 2 tbsp coconut cream

Instructions:

Beat the butter together until it has become smooth and soft. Start adding the sugar a ½ cup at a time. Mix until fluffy.

Mix in the coconut cream and vanilla, and then the peanut butter and salt until it all comes together. Pour into a baking dish and refrigerate until hard.

Remove from dish and cut into squares. Keep store in the fridge.

Easter Fudge

Ingredients:

- 2 cup coconut oil
- ¼ tsp salt
- 1 cup nut butter
- 2 tsp vanilla
- ½ cup sweetener
- Pink: 1 cup chopped beets
- Green: ½ cup dried parsley
- Purple: ¾ cup blueberries

Instructions:

Melt the coconut oil in a little pot.

Place the oil and other ingredients, except for the colorings, in your blender and combine until smooth.

Split this mixture between three bowls. Place one bowl's contents in a blender and place in one of the color ingredients. Blend until combined. Pour this into a baking dish.

Clean the blender out and repeat with the next color and drizzle it into the baking dish. Finish up by blending the last color. Once poured into the baking dish, take a knife and swirl the colors together.

Refrigerate until hard and then cut into squares.

Orange Walnut Fat Bomb

Ingredients:

- 4.5-oz 85% dark chocolate or milk chocolate if you prefer it
- 10-15 drops Stevia
- ¼ cup coconut oil
- 1 tsp cinnamon
- 1 1/3 cup walnuts, chopped
- 1 tbsp orange peel

Instructions:

Place chocolate in a double boiler and melt, and then mix in the coconut oil and cinnamon. Add however much Stevia that you want and then stir in the orange peel.

Mix in the walnuts, making sure it's well incorporated. Spoon this into muffin cups and refrigerate until firm.

Chocolate Coconut Gummies

Ingredients:

- 1 cup coconut milk, full-fat
- Stevia
- 1 tsp vanilla extract
- 3 tbsp gelatin
- A pinch of Sea salt
- 1 tbsp MCT oil
- 3 tsp cacao powder

Instructions:

Place everything in a blender and mix together. Place the mixture in a dish or candy molds.

Place in the fridge until firm and remove from the molds, or slice them into squares. Keep them in the fridge.

Chocolate Coconut Candies

Ingredients:

- ½ cup coconut butter
- ¼ tsp vanilla
- ½ cup coconut oil
- ¼ cup cocoa powder
- ½ shredded unsweetened coconut
- ¼ cup powdered Swerve
- 3 tbsp Swerve
- 1-oz unsweetened chocolate
- 1 ½-oz cocoa butter
- ¼ cup powdered Swerve

Instructions:

Set mini muffin liners in a cupcake tin.

Combine a half cup of coconut butter and coconut oil together in a saucepan until melted. Stir in coconut and three tablespoons of Swerve.

Pour this mixture into the paper liners and freeze until hard.

Stir together the chocolate and cocoa butter over a double boiler. Stir in the Swerve and cocoa powder.

Remove from heat and add the vanilla. Pour this over the coconut mixture and let it set up.

Peanut Butter Fudge 2

Ingredients:

- 2 tsp vanilla Stevia
- 1 c coconut oil
- A pinch of salt
- 1 cup peanut butter
- ¼ cup vanilla almond milk

Instructions:

Place the peanut butter and coconut oil in a pot and mix together.

Pour this into the blender along with everything else and mix until it all comes together. Line a loaf pan with parchment and pour in the mixture.

Place in the fridge for a few hours until hard and then slice.

Raspberry Cheesecake Truffles

Ingredients:

- 8-oz cream cheese, softened
- ½ cup powdered Swerve
- ¼ cup coconut oil, melted
- 2 tbsp heavy cream
- 1 ½ cup chocolate chips, sugar-free
- Red food coloring
- 1 tsp vanilla Stevia
- 3 tsp raspberry extract
- A pinch of Salt

Instructions:

Cream together the cream cheese and Swerve with a hand mixer. Add in the cream, extract, Stevia, food coloring, and salt. Slowly mix in the coconut oil.

Place in the fridge for around an hour.

With a mini cookie scoop, make 48 balls out of the batter. Place in the freezer for an hour.

Melt the chocolate and coat the balls.

Keep stored in the fridge.

Lemon Cheesecake Cups

Ingredients:

- 4 tbsp unsalted butter, softened
- ¼ coconut oil, melted
- 1 tbsp lemon zest
- 2 tsp Splenda
- 1 tsp lemon juice
- 4-oz Neufchatel cheese, softened

Instructions:

Place everything in a blender and combine together completely.

Spoon it out into muffin tins liners that are greased up and freeze until firm.

Top with extra lemon zest.

Only if you have a sour tooth

Almond Joy Balls

Ingredients:

- 2 tbsp cocoa powder
- 2 tbsp almond butter
- 1 tbsp coconut flour
- Splenda
- 2 tbsp coconut oil, melted

Instructions:

Stir together the cocoa powder and coconut oil. Mix in the almond butter until smooth, and then stir in the Splenda and coconut flour.

Once mixed, divide into fourths and roll into balls and set on wax paper to freeze for a few minutes.

Keep stored in the fridge.

Mounds Barks

Ingredients:

- 2 cup shredded coconut, unsweetened
- A pinch of sea salt
- 1 cup coconut oil
- ¼ tsp cinnamon
- 4-oz Neufchatel cheese
- 4 tsp Splenda
- 2 tbsp cocoa powder

Instructions:

Melt the oil in a pot and then mix in the cinnamon, coconut, salt, and Splenda.

Place wax paper in a square baking dish and add in the mixture. Smooth and press the mixture into a solid layer.

Freeze until firm. Melt the cream cheese and cocoa powder together and place this over the hardened coconut mixture.

Place in the freezer until firm. Cut into pieces once firm. Store in a container in the fridge.

Orange Butter Pecans

Ingredients:

- 4 pecan halves
- A pinch of Sea salt
- ½ tbsp unsalted butter
- ½ tsp orange zest
- 1-oz Neufchatel cheese

Instructions:

Toast the pecans for ten minutes at 350 and then cool completely.

Add the softened butter, cream cheese, and zest and mix until creamy. Place the mixture on top of each pecan half and sprinkle with sea salt.

Cinnamon Balls

Ingredients:

- 1 c coconut butter
- 1 tsp vanilla extract
- 1 tsp Splenda
- 1 c coconut milk
- ½ tsp cinnamon
- 1 c coconut shreds
- ½ tsp nutmeg

Instructions:

Put everything, except the shredded coconut, in a double boiler and melt together.

Put in a bowl and refrigerate until you can roll them into balls. Roll each ball in the shredded coconut.

Keep refrigerated.

Chocolate Coconut Peanut Butter Cups

Ingredients:

- ¾ c coconut oil
- Liquid Splenda
- ¼ c cocoa powder
- ¼ c peanut butter

Instructions:

Melt the coconut oil and separate between three bowls. Mix the cocoa in one bowl, and add some Splenda.

Mix the peanut butter in another bowl, and add some Splenda.

Add paper liners to cupcake tin and add the chocolate mixture in the bottom of each. Refrigerate until firm.

Pour the peanut butter mixture on top and refrigerate until set. Add the rest of the oil over the top. Keep refrigerated.

ocolate Cinnamon Peanut Butter Squares

Ingredients:

- 4 tbsp coconut oil
- A pinch of Sea salt
- 1 tsp vanilla extract
- 4 tbsp cocoa powder
- ¼ tbsp cinnamon
- 4 c chopped walnuts
- ½ c peanut butter
- 3 tsp Splenda

Instructions:

Once coconut oil is melted, stir in the cocoa, vanilla, and Splenda. Carefully fold in the nuts.

Pour into a square baking dish and spread around.

Mix together the cinnamon and peanut butter and then pour over top the chocolate. Sprinkle with sea salt.

Freeze until firm and slice into squares.

Seasonal Spice Balls

Ingredients:

- 8-oz Neufchatel cheese, softened
- 1 tsp ginger
- ¾ c coconut oil
- ½ tsp ground cloves
- ½ c Splenda
- ½ tsp nutmeg
- 1 tbsp cinnamon

Instructions:

Place everything, except oil, in a food processor. Pulse as you pour in the oil in a thin stream.

Split into sixths and roll into balls. Refrigerate until firm and top with some dark chocolate.

Keep refrigerated.

Pumpkin Butter Balls

Ingredients:

- 4 tbsp unsalted butter
- Liquid Splenda
- 2 tbsp coconut oil
- 1 stick of Cinnamon
- ½ c pumpkin
- Nutmeg spice
- 1 tsp Ginger or to taste (some people like more or less)
- 2 Garlic cloves

Instructions:

Melt the coconut oil and whisk in the butter. Keep blending as you add in the pumpkin until smooth. Mix in as much of the spices and sweetener as you like.

Drop spoonful's on parchment and refrigerate until firm.

Roll into balls once hard and keep refrigerated.

Blackberry Nut Squares

Ingredients:

- 2-oz crush macadamia
- Sweetener
- 1 c coconut oil
- 4-oz cream cheese
- ½ tsp lemon juice
- 1 c blackberries
- 1 c coconut butter
- ½ tsp vanilla
- 3 tbsp mascarpone cheese
- 1 c coconut butter

Instructions:

Place the nuts in the bottom of a casserole dish and bake at 325 until golden. Allow to cool.

Spread the cream cheese over your crust.

Mix the blackberries, coconut butter, coconut oil, vanilla, mascarpone cheese, and lemon juice together. Taste and adjust sweetener as you need.

Pour this over the cheese. Freeze an hour and slice into squares. Keep in the fridge.

Cinnabon Blond Bars

Ingredients:

1st icing:

- 1 tbsp almond butter
- 1 tbsp coconut oil

2nd icing:

- ½ tsp cinnamon
- 1 tbsp coconut oil

Bar:

- 1/8 tsp cinnamon
- ½ c coconut cream, diced

Instructions:

Place wax paper in a baking dish. Mix together the coconut cream and cinnamon and press into the dish.

Whisk the coconut oil and almond butter together and spread over the cinnamon mixture. Freeze until set.

Mix the coconut oil and cinnamon and the drizzle over the bars and freeze until set.

Slice into bars and enjoy.

Peppermint Cups

Ingredients:

- ¾ c coconut butter
- ½ tsp peppermint extract
- 1/3 c shredded coconut, unsweetened
- 2 tsp cocoa powder
- 3 tbsp coconut oil

Instructions:

Mix the peppermint extract, coconut butter, shredded coconut, and a tablespoon of coconut oil together. Pour into muffin liners to half full. Refrigerate until hard.

Mix the rest of the oil and cocoa powder together and pour over the hard peppermint mixture. Refrigerate until hard.

Keep refrigerated.

Allspice Almond Squares

Ingredients:

- 1 tbsp coconut oil
- 2 tbsp almond butter
- 1 tsp cocoa powder
- 4 drops liquid Splenda
- 1 tbsp heavy cream
- ¼ tsp allspice

Instructions:

Press the almond butter into a square container. Blend the allspice, coconut oil, cocoa powder, and heavy cream together and pour on top.

Freeze two hours and take out of the container, top with almonds.

Crave Buster

Ingredients:

- 1 c coconut oil, melted
- 1 c almond butter
- 1 c cacao powder

Instructions:

Whisk all of the ingredients together until no lumps remain. Pour a half tablespoon of the mixture into 32 mini muffin cups.

Freeze until hard and keep refrigerated.

Blackberry Coconut

Ingredients:

- 1 c coconut butter
- 1 tbsp lemon juice
- 1 c coconut oil
- ½ tsp vanilla
- ½ c blackberries
- ½ tsp Stevia drops

Instructions:

Stir together the oil, blackberries, and coconut butter in a pot until mixed well. Add this, and the others in your blender and mix together.

Place into a parchment lined pan and refrigerate until hard. Slice into squares and keep refrigerated.

Vanilla Fat Bombs

Ingredients:

- 2 tbsp. powdered Swerve
- 1 vanilla bean
- ¼ c butter
- 10-15 drops liquid Stevia
- ¼ c extra virgin coconut oil
- 1 c macadamia nuts, unsalted

Instructions:

Put macadamia nuts into food processor and process until smooth. Put in a bowl and add softened butter and coconut oil. Mix well. Add Stevia, vanilla bean, and powdered Swerve. Stir to combine. Pour into mini muffin forms. Put about one and a half tablespoons in each. Place in the refrigerator about 30 minutes and take out of mold. Store in an airtight containers in the fridge.

Coconut Fat Bombs

Ingredients:

- A pinch of Salt
- 1 ½ c shredded coconut, unsweetened
- ¼ tsp cinnamon
- ¼ c extra virgin coconut oil
- ¼ c butter

Instructions:

Warm oven to 350F. Place coconut on a baking sheet in an even layer. Bake for eight minutes until slightly browned. Stir a few times, so it won't burn. Put in a food processor and process mix until smooth.

Mix in the butter and coconut oil. Mix well. Add in salt, cinnamon, and Stevia if you like it sweeter. Mix again. Pour into mini muffin forms and place in the fridge about 30 minutes. When done, take out of forms and place in the refrigerator.

Fat Bombs

Ingredients:

Filling:

- 1 tbsp. lemon zest
- 8 tbsp. coconut oil
- 1 c Swerve
- ½ c lemon juice
- 1 c Swerve

Coating:

- ¼ tsp sea salt
- 1 tsp lemon extract
- 2/3 c Swerve
- 4 oz. cocoa butter

Instructions:

Using a double boiler, melt cocoa butter. This takes longer than normal fats. When melted, add in sweetener, salt, and extracts. Place into 24 truffle molds. Put in the freezer.

Filling: Add lemon zest, lemon juice, eggs, and sweetener to saucepan. Whisk in coconut oil. Constantly whisk until mixture begins to thicken and coats back of the spoon. Be careful to not let it boil. This will take about 12 minutes. Strain mixture into a bowl. Set this into a bowl of ice water. Mix to cool off.

Make truffles: Remove mold from freezer. Add lemon curd to all molds. Add extra coating to bottom, so the curd is covered with the coating. Freeze until set.

Coconut Chocolate Fat Bombs

Ingredients:

- 1 c shredded coconut
- 1 c coconut butter
- 1 tsp Stevia
- 1 c coconut milk, full fat
- 4 tbsp. cocoa powder
- 1 tsp vanilla

Instructions:

Using a double boiler, mix all ingredients except shredded coconut. Stir until melted and well combined. Take off heat. Refrigerate until you can roll it into balls. Roll into about 12 balls and then in the shredded coconut.

Fudgy Macadamia Fat Bombs

Ingredients:

- ¼ c coconut oil
- 2 oz. cocoa butter
- 4 oz. chopped macadamias
- 2 tbsp. cocoa powder, unsweetened
- 2 tbsp. Swerve

Instructions:

Melt cocoa butter and add cocoa powder. Stir until well combined. Using a double boiler works really well. Add in Swerve until completely combined.

Add in cream and nuts. Stir to combine. Pour into six paper molds. Let cool and put in the refrigerator.

Chocolate Almond Fat Bombs

Ingredients:

- 10 to 15 almonds
- 1 c almond butter
- Stevia, to taste
- 1 c coconut oil
- ¼ c coconut flour
- ½ c cacao powder

Instructions:

Melt coconut and almond oil together in the pot. Add in the cacao powder, Stevia, and coconut flour. Stir to combine.

Let cool and roll into about 15 balls.

Put an almond in each ball and store in the refrigerator.

Chocolate and Vanilla Fat Bombs

Ingredients:

- ¼ c 100% dark chocolate
- 1 tbsp. vanilla extract
- 1 c coconut butter
- Stevia, to taste
- 1 c coconut milk
- 1 c shredded coconut, unsweetened

Instructions:

Place coconut milk and butter into a pot and melt.

Add remaining ingredients, except chocolate.

Stir well to combine and place in the refrigerator for two hours.

Roll into balls and put back in the refrigerator until hard. This will take about three hours.

Melt dark chocolate and dip each ball into chocolate. Store in the refrigerator.

Peppermint Patties

Ingredients:

- ½ c coconut butter
- 4 tbsp. coconut oil
- 2 tbsp. raw honey
- ¼ c shredded unsweetened coconut
- 4 oz. 100% dark chocolate
- 2 tbsp. coconut oil
- 1 tsp peppermint extract

Instructions:

Soften two tablespoons coconut oil and coconut butter. Mix in peppermint, honey, and shredded coconut.

Put two teaspoons mixture in bottom of mini muffin cups. Place in refrigerator for one hour. This needs to be solid before continuing.

Melt dark chocolate with four tablespoons coconut oil and mix well. Place one teaspoon of chocolate in each of the mini muffin cups. Put back in the refrigerator for another hour. When solid, repeat the process until all ingredients have been used.

Jalapeno Popper Eggs

Ingredients:

- ¼ tsp smoked paprika
- 6 eggs
- 2 oz. cream cheese, softened
- 16 pickled jalapeno slices, divided
- 4 to 6 tbsp. mayonnaise
- 6 slices bacon, cooked and crumbled

Instructions:

Hard boil eggs, cool in an ice bath, peel.

Chop up four jalapeno slice and set aside. Slice eggs in half lengthwise. Remove the yolks and mash together. Stir in jalapenos, mayonnaise, cream cheese, and bacon. Be sure all are mixed well. Put mixture in a baggie and snip off the corner. Squeeze mixture into each egg. Top each egg with a jalapeno slice. Sprinkle with paprika.

Guacamole Deviled Eggs

Ingredients:

- Cayenne pepper
- 1 large avocado
- 6 eggs
- ½ tsp garlic salt
- 4 strips bacon, cooked and crumbled
- 1 tbsp. onion flakes
- 1 tbsp. minced garlic
- 1 tbsp. onion flakes
- 2 tbsp. salsa
- 1 tbsp. lime juice

Instructions:

Hard boil eggs. Cool. Peel. Mash up avocado In a large bowl. Cut the eggs in half. Carefully take out the yolks and put with the avocado. Add cayenne, garlic salt, onion, lime juice, garlic, salsa, and bacon. Mix well until all ingredients are well incorporated. Put in a baggie and snip off the corner. Squeeze mixture into egg whites.

Pistachio, Bacon, Braunschweiger Truffles

Ingredients:

- 8 slices bacon, cooked and finely chopped
- 8 oz. Braunschweiger, room temp
- 1 tsp Dijon mustard
- ¼ c chopped pistachio
- 6 oz. softened cream cheese

Instructions:

Put the pistachios and braunschweiger in a food processor. Mix well. Whisk the cream cheese in a different bowl with mustard until smooth. Roll braunschweiger into 12 balls. Cover each ball with some cream cheese mixture. This will be very messy. Put on a baking sheet and chill for 30 minutes. When chilled, roll balls in the chopped bacon. Store in the refrigerator.

Buffalo Chicken Deviled Eggs

Ingredients:

- 2 tbsp. blue cheese dressing
- 6 eggs, hard boiled
- 1 celery rib, chopped
- 6 oz. chicken, chopped and cooked
- ¼ c buffalo sauce
- ¼ onion
- ¼ c blue cheese crumbles

Instructions:

Peel eggs and slice in half lengthwise. Take the yolks and place in a bowl. Mix in all the rest of the ingredients. Put mixture into a plastic bowl. Snip off one corner and pipe into each egg white. Store in the fridge.

Bacon Mozzarella Sticks

Ingredients:

- Coconut oil
- Pack mozzarella sticks, sliced in half
- 24 bacon slices

Instructions:

Heat coconut oil in a deep fryer. Wrap bacon around each cheese stick half. Secure bacon with a toothpick. Drop into oil and cook a couple minutes until crispy. Drain on paper towels. Remove the toothpicks and enjoy.

Salmon Fat Bombs

Ingredients:

- A pinch of Salt
- 1 tbsp. lemon juice
- ½ c cream cheese, full fat
- 2 tbsp. chopped dill
- 1/3 c butter
- ½ package salmon

Instructions:

Add salmon, cream cheese, dill, lemon juice, and butter to food processor. Process until smooth. Put parchment paper On the baking sheet. Using two tablespoons of mixture for each fat bomb. Sprinkle with dill and refrigerate until firm. Keep in a container in the fridge.

Cheesy Jalapeno Fat Bombs

Ingredients:

- 2 jalapenos, seeded and chopped
- 3.5 oz. full fat cream cheese
- ¼ c cheddar cheese, grated
- ¼ c ghee, room temp
- 4 slices bacon

Instructions:

Mash ghee and cream cheese together. Put the oven at 325. Put parchment paper onto a baking sheet. Put bacon On the baking sheet and bake 25 minutes until crispy. Remove bacon and let cool. When cool, crumble and set aside.

Mix the bacon grease, jalapenos, and cheddar cheese to cream cheese mixture. Refrigerate for 30 minutes. Form into six balls and roll in bacon. Refrigerate for about a week.

Pizza Fat Bombs

Ingredients:

- Pepper
- 4 oz. cream cheese
- 2 tbsp. sun-dried tomato pesto
- A pinch of Salt
- 14 pepperoni slices
- 2 tbsp. chopped basil
- 8 black olives

Instructions:

Dice up olives and pepperoni. Combine cream cheese, basil, and pesto until mixed well. Stir in pepperoni and olives. Form into six balls. Garnish with extra olives, basil, and pepperoni.

Mediterranean Fat Bombs

Ingredients:

- 5 tbsp. parmesan cheese, grated
- ½ c full-fat cream cheese
- ¼ tsp salt
- ¼ c ghee
- Pepper
- 3 tbsp. chopped fresh herbs
- 2 crushed garlic cloves
- 4 sun dried tomatoes
- 4 olives

Instructions:

When ghee and cream cheese are soft, mash together. Mix in olives and tomatoes. Stir in pepper, salt, garlic, and herbs. When combined, place in the refrigerator for 20 to 30 minutes. Put parmesan in a bowl. Form cream cheese mixture into five balls and roll in parmesan cheese. Store in the refrigerator.

Bacon and Guacamole Fat Bombs

Ingredients:

- 4 bacon slices
- ½ avocado
- 2 tbsp. chopped cilantro
- ¼ c ghee, room temp
- ¼ tsp salt
- 2 crushed garlic cloves
- A pinch of Pepper
- 1 small chili pepper, chopped
- 1 tbsp. lime juice
- ½ onion, diced

Instructions:

Cook bacon and let cool. Mix lime juice, garlic, cilantro, chili pepper, avocado, and ghee. Season with salt and pepper. Mash with potato masher and add in onion. Mix the bacon grease in and stir to combine. Cover with foil and refrigerate about 30 minutes. Crumble up the bacon. Take guacamole out of the fridge and form into six balls. Roll in bacon. Store in the refrigerator.

Bacon Maple Squares

Ingredients:

- 8 oz. Neufchatel cheese, softened
- ¼ c sugar-free maple syrup
- ½ c unsalted butter
- 8 cooked and crumbled bacon slices
- 4 tsp bacon fat
- 4 tbsp. coconut oil

Instructions:

Mix all ingredients together. Keep some bacon out. Melt everything in the microwave in ten-second intervals until smooth.

Pour into square dish and place in the freezer to get firm. Remove and sprinkle with crumbled bacon. Slice into squares and serve.

Bacon and Egg Fat Bombs

Ingredients:

- 4 bacon slices
- 2 eggs
- ¼ tsp salt
- ¼ c softened ghee
- A pinch of Pepper
- 2 tbsp. mayonnaise

Instructions:

Cook bacon in a 375-degree oven for 10 to 15 minutes. Let cool. Hard boil eggs. Put cooked eggs in an ice bath until cooled. Peel. Put ghee in a bowl. Quarter eggs and add them to the ghee. Mash. Add in mayonnaise, pepper, and salt. Add bacon grease and mix well. Refrigerate for about 30 minutes. You should be able to form into balls.

Crumble bacon. Form egg mixture into six balls and roll in bacon crumbles. Keep refrigerated.

Vanilla Raspberry Smoothie

Ingredients:

- Whipped cream
- ½ c raspberries
- 1 tbsp. Swerve
- ½ c mascarpone cheese
- 1 tbsp. MCT oil
- ¼ c water
- ½ tsp vanilla extract
- 5 ice cubes

Instructions:

Place everything, minus whipped cream, in a blender. Mix until completely smooth. Add some whipped cream on top if you want.

Vanilla Smoothie

Ingredients:

- Whipped cream
- 2 egg yolks
- 1 tbsp Swerve
- ½ c mascarpone cheese
- 1 tsp vanilla extract
- ¼ c water
- 1 tbsp coconut oil
- 5 ice cubes

Instructions:

Put Swerve, vanilla, coconut oil, mascarpone, ice, water, and egg yolks in a blender. Blend until smooth. Top with whipped cream.

If you don't eat eggs, you can still do this but replace the eggs with a tablespoon of chia seeds.

Keto Coffee

Ingredients:

- 1 tbsp Swerve
- 1 c brewed coffee
- 3 egg yolks
- 1 tbsp coconut milk
- ½ tsp cinnamon
- 1 tbsp MCT oil
- 1 tbsp coconut oil

Instructions:

Put egg yolks, coconut oil, cinnamon, coconut milk, MCT oil, and coffee into a blender. Blend until smooth and frothy. Add Swerve if you like your coffee sweet.

White Hot Chocolate

Ingredients:

- Liquid Stevia, to taste
- ½ c coconut milk
- 1 tbsp coconut oil
- ½ c water
- 1 oz. white chocolate
- ¼ tsp vanilla extract
- 1 tbsp Swerve
- A pinch of Salt

Instructions:

Put Swerve, vanilla, salt, water, and coconut milk into a small pot. Let come to boil, stirring often. When bubbles begin to form, take off heat. Mix in coconut oil and white chocolate until melted. Add Stevia if it needs to be sweeter. Use a hand blender to make it frothy and smooth.

Herbal Coffee

Ingredients:

- 1 tsp coconut cream
- 2 c fresh herbal coffee
- 1 tsp ghee
- 1 tsp coconut oil

Instructions:

Mix everything in the blender until frothy.

Serve into a nice coffee mug.

Bulletproof Coffee Drops

Ingredients:

- ½ c ghee
- ¼ tsp salt
- 1 c coconut oil, melted
- ½ tsp cinnamon

Instructions:

Melt coconut oil and ghee together. Add cinnamon and salt. Mix well to combine. Pour into nine spots of an ice cube tray. Freeze and remove from the tray. Keep in a container in the fridge until you are ready for them.

To use, put ten ounces of coffee and one cube into the blender and blend until combined and foamy.

Pumpkin Cheesecake Squares

Ingredients:

- 2 tbsp Splenda
- ½ c unsalted butter
- 1/8 tsp sea salt
- 3 oz. Neufchatel cheese
- ½ tsp pumpkin spice
- ½ c pumpkin puree
- 1 tsp cinnamon
- ¼ c chopped pecans
- 2 tbsp vanilla extract

Instructions:

Melt butter in the pot on the stove. Add pumpkin and stir constantly. Add cream cheese, pecans, spices, and Splenda. Whisk until smooth. Add vanilla. Stir to combine.

Take off heat. Line 9-inch square pan with waxed paper and pour mixture into pan.

Sprinkle with pecans and put in the freezer for 24 hours.

When ready to slice, take out waxed paper. Slice into squares.

Keep in an airtight container in the freezer.

Vanilla Mocha Pops

Ingredients:

- ¾ tsp liquid Splenda
- 1 ½ tbsp. cocoa powder
- 4 tbsp unsalted butter
- ½ tsp vanilla extract
- ½ tsp coffee extract
- 2 tbsp heavy cream
- 4 tbsp coconut oil

Instructions:

For the vanilla layer: Melt butter in the microwave. Add heavy cream. Stir to combine. Let cool.

Once cool, add vanilla and stir.

For mocha layer: Mix sweetener, coffee extract, coconut oil, and cocoa powder.

Pour the vanilla mixture into muffin tins that have been lined with paper liners. Place in the fridge until firm.

When firm, take out of the fridge and pour in the mocha mixture.

Place plastic wrap over them and stick popsicle sticks through. Freeze 30 minutes.

Optional topping. Pour a thin layer of melted dark chocolate before freezing.

Chocolate Peanut Butter Pops

Ingredients:

- ¼ c chopped walnuts
- ½ c coconut oil
- A pinch of Salt
- ½ c peanut butter
- 2 oz. softened cream cheese
- 1/3 c whey protein powder, vanilla
- 1/3 c cocoa powder
- ½ tsp vanilla extract
- Liquid sweetener that equals 1 c sugar

Instructions:

Grease 5 x 7 baking dish and line with waxed paper. Leave some hanging out to remove fudge later. Grease waxed paper.

Melt peanut butter and coconut oil together in the saucepan. They need to be mixed well. In another bowl, beat cream cheese until soft. Add peanut butter and mix until smooth. Add sugar and vanilla. Combine until smooth.

In a different bowl, whisk salt, protein powder, and cocoa powder. Sift the dry ingredients into the wet and beat until smooth. Fold in nuts, if using. Spread into the prepared pan and freeze until set. Take out and cut into 20 squares. Put back into the freezer to keep cold.

Peanut Butter Chocolate Ice Cream Bites

Ingredients:

For Ice Cream

- 3 tbsp vanilla syrup, sugar-free
- ½ c heavy whipping cream

For Outside

- 4 tbsp chunky peanut butter
- 4 oz. cream cheese
- 1 pack chocolate pudding, sugar-free
- 8 oz. low carb chocolate shake

Instructions:

Combine chocolate shake and cream cheese with electric mixer until smooth. Mix in pudding and peanut butter. This will be very thick. On the baking sheet lined with waxed paper, spread mixture in a thin layer with a rubber spatula. Put in the freezer until almost hard. This will be about 40 minutes. Check at the 20-minute mark to be sure it isn't hard. It will need to be pliable for the next step.

While chocolate is cooling, combine vanilla syrup and whipping cream until stiff peaks have formed. Drop spoonful's of the ice cream mixture onto waxed paper. Put in the freezer until solid.

Remove chocolate and slice into squares that are the same number of spoonful's of ice cream you have. The squares need to be big enough to wrap around ice cream. Take squares and wrap them around the ice cream and put back into the freezer.

Neapolitan Fat Bomb

Ingredients:

- ½ c butter
- 2 strawberries
- ½ c coconut oil
- 1 tsp vanilla
- ½ c sour cream
- 2 tbsp cocoa powder
- ½ c cream cheese
- 25 drops Stevia
- 2 tbsp erythritol

Instructions:

Mix Stevia, cream cheese, erythritol, coconut oil, sour cream, and butter. Using an immersion blender to combine the ingredients. Divide into three bowls. In one bowl add cocoa powder. Another put the vanilla. The last one gets the strawberries.

Using the immersion blender, mix the ingredients in each bowl together. Rinse off after each use. Put the chocolate mixture in the bottom of square molds. Freeze 30 minutes. Repeat with vanilla and last strawberry. Remember to freeze 30 minutes between each layer. This time freeze for one hour. When completely frozen, unmold and store in an airtight container in the fridge.

Tiramisu Ice Bomb

Ingredients:

- 1 oz. cacao butter
- 1 ¼ c creamed coconut milk
- ¼ oz. 90% dark chocolate
- ¼ c Swerve
- Liquid Stevia, to taste
- 2 tsp rum extract
- ¼ c chilled coffee

Instructions:

Put coffee, rum extract, coconut milk, and Swerve in the food processor and process until smooth. Taste, if it needs more sweetener, add Stevia and pulse some more.

Put two tablespoons of coffee mixture into 12 mini muffin molds. Freeze about two hours. Melt the cacao butter and dark chocolate in a double boiler. Cool slightly. Put a toothpick into each ice bomb. Hold over the bowl of chocolate and spoon some chocolate over. Be sure to coat entire ball. Put the ball on a parchment lined baking sheet. Freeze for 15 minutes. Remove toothpicks. Store in an airtight container in the freezer.

Mocha Ice Bombs

Ingredients:

- 1 oz. cocoa butter, melted
- 1 c cream cheese
- 2.5 oz. 90% chocolate, melted
- ¼ c powdered sweetener
- ¼ c coffee, chilled
- 2 tbsp cocoa, unsweetened

Instructions:

Put sweetener, cream cheese, cocoa, and coffee in the food processor and mix until smooth. Roll two tablespoons of the mixture into a ball and put On the baking sheet covered with parchment paper and freeze.

Mix melted cocoa butter and chocolate together and roll each ice bomb in the chocolate. Freeze two more hours, until set.

Shrimp and Artichoke Dip

Ingredients:

- ½ c sour cream
- 1 tsp garlic powder
- 6 oz. pre-cooked shrimp
- 6 green onions, chopped
- 1 tsp red pepper flakes
- 1 ¼ c shredded parmesan cheese
- 14 oz. can quartered artichoke hearts
- 1 tbsp minced garlic
- 2 tbsp butter
- 1 c shredded cheddar cheese
- ½ c mayonnaise

Instructions:

Put oven on 350. Remove tails and chop shrimp. Sauté with red pepper flakes and butter for ten minutes. Chop artichoke hearts. In a large bowl, add all ingredients and mix until thoroughly combined. Pour into baking dish and bake 30 minutes until bubbly and golden brown.

Caramelized Onion and Bacon Dip

Ingredients:

- 2 sprigs parsley
- 2 large onions
- 2 tbsp cooking sherry
- 10 sliced bacon
- 2 tbsp salted butter
- 8 oz. softened cream cheese
- 2 tbsp minced garlic
- ¾ c sour cream
- ¼ c shredded parmesan cheese

Instructions:

Put sherry, olive oil, garlic, and butter in a skillet. Mix in onions and cook on low heat until caramelized. This is going to take about 30 minutes. In a different pan, cook bacon until crispy. Place on paper towels to drain. Cool completely. When cooled, crumble. in a bowl, put parsley, parmesan, sour cream, and cream cheese. Mix to combine. When onions have cooled completely, put them and bacon into the cream cheese mixture. Stir well to combine.

Macadamia Chocolate Fudge

Ingredients:

- ¼ c heavy cream
- 2 oz. cocoa butter
- 4 oz. chopped macadamias
- 2 tbsp unsweetened cocoa powder
- 2 tbsp Swerve

Instructions:

Melt the cocoa butter in a double boiler. Mix in the Swerve and cocoa powder. Mix well until ingredients are melted and well combined. Add macadamias and stir again. Add cream, stir again. If needed, warm it up to get everything well combined. Pour into paper lines. Cool on the counter top. When cooled, place in the refrigerator to harden. Store in an airtight container at room temperature. This has a soft chocolate consistency.

Valentine's Day Keto Bombs

Ingredients:

- 2 oz. almond butter
- 2 oz. coconut oil
- 8 drops EZ-Sweetz
- 1 oz. cream cheese
- 2 oz. 85% dark chocolate
- ½ oz. Torani sugar-free vanilla syrup
- 1 tsp cocoa powder

Instructions:

Put all ingredients except almond butter in glass pourable measuring cup. Microwave 30 seconds. Stir, if not melted, microwave and stir again. When smooth, pour enough to coat the bottom of the mold. Using a spoon place a dollop of almond butter on top. Pour more chocolate over almond butter. Place in the freezer until hard. When hard, unmold, and enjoy. Store in an airtight container in the refrigerator.

White Chocolate Coconut Fudge

Ingredients:

- A pinch of Salt
- 4 oz. cacao butter
- 1 tsp coconut liquid Stevia
- 1 can coconut milk
- 1 tsp vanilla
- ½ c coconut oil
- ½ c vanilla protein powder
- 1 c coconut butter

Instructions:

Melt cacao butter in the saucepan. Add coconut butter, oil, and milk. Stir to combine. Stir until no lumps are left. Take off heat. Whisk in Stevia, salt, protein powder, and vanilla extract. Put parchment paper in an 8 X 8-inch baking pan. Pour into prepared pan. Add coconut flakes to top if desired. Refrigerate four hours or overnight. This can be stored at room temperature.

Valentine Hearts

Ingredients:

- 3.5 oz. 85% dark chocolate
- Sweetener of choice
- ¼ c freeze-dried strawberry powder
- 7.1 oz. pkg. creamed coconut

Instructions:

Melt creamed coconut using a double boiler. Stirring constantly. Add strawberry powder and mix well. This will sweeten the mixture. If it needs to be sweeter, add sweetener of choice. Spoon into heart shaped molds. Place in the fridge until firm. Melt chocolate. When coconut hearts are hard, remove from the molds. Dip into melted chocolate and cover completely. Place on parchment paper to harden. Place back in the fridge until chocolate is set. These can be stored at room temperature. If they begin to get soft, place back in the fridge.

Ginger Cups

Ingredients:

- 1 tsp ginger
- 1/3 c softened coconut butter
- 1 tsp granulated sweetener of choice
- 1/3 c softened coconut oil
- 1 oz. unsweetened shredded coconut

Instructions:

Put all the ingredients in a bowl and mix until sweetener is dissolved. Pour into molds and refrigerate for ten minutes. Store in an airtight container in the fridge.

Chocolate Almond Truffles

Ingredients:

- 10 to 15 whole almonds
- 1 c almond butter
- Stevia to taste
- 1 c coconut oil
- ¼ c coconut flour
- ½ c cacao powder

Instructions:

Melt coconut oil and almond butter in the saucepan. Add Stevia, coconut flour, and cacao powder. Mix well to combine. Let cool. Form into 10 to 15 ping pong size balls. Put an almond in the middle of each. Put in refrigerator to set. Store in an airtight container in the refrigerator.

English Toffee Fat Bombs

Ingredients:

- 3 tbsp sugar-free English Toffee syrup
- 1 c coconut oil
- ½ c peanut butter
- 2 tbsp butter
- ¾ tbsp. cocoa powder
- 4 oz. cream cheese

Instructions:

Put all ingredients in the saucepan. Stir until everything is melted and smooth. Pour into molds. Place in the freezer for a couple of hours. Take out of the mold. Store in an airtight container in the freezer.

Orange Cardamom Walnut Truffles

Ingredients:

- ½ c unsweetened shredded coconut
- 1 c almond or walnut butter
- Stevia to taste
- ¼ c coconut oil
- 1 tsp cacao powder
- 2 tsp orange zest
- Dash of cardamom
- 1/3 c walnuts
- ¼ c unsweetened coconut flakes

Instructions:

Put all ingredients in a blender except the shredded coconut. Blend well. Place in the freezer to firm up. Form small balls from the mixture. Roll the balls in the shredded coconut. Place in the refrigerator to set hard. Store in an airtight container in the refrigerator.

Spiced Refrigerator Candy

Ingredients:

- ½ tsp ground nutmeg
- ¾ c coconut oil
- 1 tsp grated ginger
- 8 oz. full-fat cream cheese, warmed
- ½ c Swerve
- ½ tsp ground cloves
- 1 tsp ground cinnamon

Instructions:

Warm the cream cheese. Place all ingredients, except coconut oil, in the food processor. Process while pouring in the coconut oil slowly. It will start to look like mayonnaise. The consistency will be like cheesecake. Divide into six individual bowls with lids. Refrigerate. Enjoy. Store any leftovers in the fridge.

Orange and Walnut Chocolate Fat Bombs

Ingredients:

- 10 to 15 drops Stevia
- 4.4 oz. 85% dark chocolate
- 1 tsp cinnamon
- ¼ c coconut oil
- ½ to 1 tbsp orange zest or orange extract
- 1 1/3 c chopped walnuts

Instructions:

Melt chocolate using a double boiler. Add cinnamon and coconut oil. Stir to combine. If needed, add Stevia. Add in orange zest or orange extract. Add walnuts and stir well. Spoon into paper cups or molds. Put in the refrigerator for two hours. Store at room temperature.

Spiced Cocoa Coolers

Ingredients:

- 15 to 20 drops Stevia
- ¼ tsp cayenne pepper
- 1 c heavy cream
- 1 tsp vanilla extract
- 2 tbsp Swerve
- 2 tbsp unsweetened cocoa powder
- 1 tsp cinnamon

Instructions:

Ingredients: will dissolve faster if the heavy cream is warmed up. Place rest of ingredients in cream and stir to combine. Pour into ice cube tray or molds. Place in the freezer for two hours. Unmold. Store in an airtight container in the freezer.

Pecan Fudge Fat Bombs

Ingredients:

- ½ c chopped pecans
- 4 oz. food grade cocoa butter
- 1/3 c heavy cream
- ½ c coconut oil
- 4 tbsp Swerve
- 4 tbsp unsweetened cocoa powder

Instructions:

Melt coconut oil and butter in a double boiler. Whisk in cocoa powder until no lumps remain. Put in a blender. Add Swerve and blend for two minutes. Add cream and blend for five minutes. The sugar needs to be dissolved. Place pecans into molds and pour chocolate over. Chill in the refrigerator for four hours. Take out of molds. Store in the refrigerator.

Blueberry Pops

Ingredients:

- 2 c 95% fat-free whipped topping
- 2 c fresh blueberries
- 6 tbsp powdered Swerve
- ½ c full-fat cream cheese

Instructions:

Puree sugar, cream cheese, and blueberries in blender until smooth and creamy. Fold in whipped topping. Spoon into ice cube trays. Freeze until hard. Put the bottom of trays in warm water for a few seconds to help release the pops.

Strawberry Peeps

Ingredients:

- ¼ c sugar equivalent
- 4 tbsp butter
- 3 regular sized strawberries
- 4 tbsp coconut oil
- 2 oz. heavy cream

Instructions:

Dice up strawberries and place in a bowl. Add heavy cream. Blend until smooth with the immersion blender. Melt butter in the microwave. If using granulated sugar, add now. Set aside. Measure the coconut oil and set to the side. Add sweetener if not already. Use the immersion blender to combine all ingredients. Place in a piping bag. Pipe into molds. Freeze for 20 minutes. Unmold and place in an airtight container. Store in the freezer.

Coconut Fat Bomb

Ingredients:

- 2 c shredded coconut, unsweetened
- ½ tsp vanilla
- 1/3 c coconut oil, melted
- 4-oz dark chocolate chips
- 2 tbsp honey

Instructions:

Put everything, except chocolate, in a blender and mix until crumbly. Form into tablespoon balls and place on wax paper. Freeze ten minutes.

Melt the chocolate and drizzle over the fat bombs. Keep in the fridge.

White Chocolate

Ingredients:

- ¼ c cocoa butter
- 10 drops vanilla Stevia
- ¼ c coconut oil

Instructions:

Melt the cocoa butter and coconut oil together. Set off the heat and mix in the sweetener. Pour the mixture into eight silicone molds, don't fill to the top.

Place in the fridge until hard. Remove from the mold and keep refrigerated.

White Chocolate Coconut

Ingredients:

- 4-oz cacao butter
- A pinch of salt
- 15-oz coconut milk
- 1 tsp coconut liquid Stevia
- ½ coconut oil
- 1 tsp vanilla
- 1 c coconut butter
- ½ c vanilla protein powder

Instructions:

Melt the cacao butter. Stir in the coconut milk, coconut butter, and coconut oil until no lumps.

Turn off the heat and stir in the protein powder, salt, vanilla, and Stevia. Pour the mixture into a square baking dish lined with parchment.

Add some coconut flakes and refrigerate until hardened.

Slice into squares and keep in the fridge.

Peppermint Mocha

Ingredients:

- ¾ c coconut butter, melted
- 2 tbsp cocoa powder
- 5-8 drops liquid Stevia
- ¼ tsp peppermint extract
- 3 tbsp coconut oil, melted
- 3 tbsp hemp seeds

Instructions:

Mix together the coconut butter, a tablespoon of coconut oil, hemp seeds, and peppermint extract.

Pour into silicone molds three-quarters full. Refrigerate until hard.

Stir together the rest of the oil, cocoa powder, and Stevia. Drizzle this in the molds.

Place back in the fridge. Remove from the mold once hard and keep stored in the fridge.

German Chocolate Fudge

Ingredients:

- 4-oz butter, softened
- 1 c coconut, unsweetened
- 1 tsp vanilla
- 4-oz coconut oil, room temp
- 1 c pecans
- 8-oz cream cheese, softened
- A pinch of salt
- 6 tbsp cocoa powder, unsweetened
- ¼ c Swerve

Instructions:

Your oven should be at 350. Put the pecans On the baking sheet and cook six minutes.

Mix everything together, except for the pecans and coconut. Whip for four to five minutes. It should be fluffy.

Mix in the pecans and coconut. The batter will become loose from the warm pecans. Pour this into a baking dish and sprinkle with extra pecans and coconut.

Place in the fridge to set and then slice into squares. Keep in the fridge.

Snickerdoodle

Ingredients:

Coating:

- 2 tbsp erythritol
- 1 tsp cinnamon

Cookie:

- 2 c almond flour
- ½ c butter, softened
- ¾ c erythritol
- ½ tsp baking soda
- A pinch of salt

Instructions:

Your oven needs to be at 350F.

Put all of the ingredients, except for the coating, in a bowl and combine. Roll it into 16 balls.

Mix the coating ingredients together and roll the cookies in them.

Flatten slightly and place on cookie sheet, bake 15 minutes. Let cool a bit and place in a bowl. They don't have to be refrigerated.

Chocolate Coconut

Ingredients:

- 2 c coconut oil
- A pinch of salt
- ½ c raw cacao powder
- 2 tsp vanilla
- 6 tbsp raw honey

Instructions:

Put all of the ingredients into your food processor and mix everything together. Taste and add more salt or honey as you need.

Dollop the mixture onto parchment paper, and place in the fridge until hard.

Keep refrigerated.

Chocolate Chip Cookie Dough

Ingredients:

- 4-oz baking chips
- 1/3 c Swerve
- ½ c butter, salted
- 1 tsp vanilla
- 8-oz cream cheese, softened
- ½ c peanut butter

Instructions:

Put all the ingredients in a bowl and cream together. Refrigerate for about 30 minutes. Use a cookie scoop, and scoop our 20 cookies on parchment paper.

Refrigerate for 30 minutes until solid. Keep refrigerated.

Fudge

Ingredients:

- 1 c nut butter
- A pinch of salt
- 1 c coconut oil
- ¼ tsp powdered Stevia
- ½ c cocoa powder, unsweetened
- 1/3 coconut flour

Instructions:

Melt together the nut butter and coconut oil in a pot. Whisk all the remaining ingredients.

Pour into a bowl and freeze for 20-25 minutes. Form the mixture into balls. Rinse your hands in cold water often to prevent the oil from melting.

Place the balls in the freezer for 10-15 minutes, and then keep them in the fridge.

Peanut Butter Fluff

Ingredients:

- ½ c heavy whipping cream
- ½ square unsweetened chocolate
- 4-oz cream cheese
- 3-4 packets Stevia
- 2 tbsp peanut butter
- ½ tsp peanut butter

Instructions:

Whip the cream until forms stiff peaks. Beat together the cream cheese, Stevia, peanut butter, and vanilla.

Fold together the cream cheese mixture and the whipping cream carefully.

Grate the chocolate over the top.

It should stay refrigerated.

Peppermint

Ingredients:

- ½ c coconut oil, melted
- 2 tbsp unsweetened cocoa
- 1 tbsp sweetener
- ¼ tsp peppermint extract

Instructions:

Stir together the coconut oil, peppermint, and sweetener. Pour this into the bottom half of six silicon molds, and make sure you only use half of the coconut mixture. Set in the fridge to set up.

Mix the cocoa into the remaining coconut oil. Pour this into the molds once the first layer is set.

Keep in the fridge until firm, and then remove from the mold. Keep stored in the fridge.

Red Velvet

Ingredients:

- 3.5 oz 90% dark chocolate
- 1/3 c whipped heavy cream
- 4.4 oz cream cheese
- 4 drops red food coloring
- 3.5 oz butter
- 1 tsp vanilla
- 3 tbsp Natvia

Instructions:

Melt the chocolate using a double boiler. As the chocolate melts, use a hand mixer and beat the rest of the ingredients together for three minutes on medium.

Switch to low, and slowly add in the chocolate and mix for two more minutes. Pour into a piping bag and pipe circles on parchment paper. Refrigerate for 40 minutes. Top with some whipped cream.

Keep in the fridge.

Chocolate Cherry

Ingredients:

- ¼ c coconut oil, melted
- ¾ c frozen sweet cherries, thawed
- ¼ c coconut butter, melted
- ½ tsp vanilla
- 3 tbsp cacao powder
- ½ tsp almond extract
- 5 drops Stevia

Instructions:

Mix together all of the ingredients, except for the cherries. Mash the cherries up and then stir them and their juices into the chocolate.

Put a tablespoon of this in mini cupcake liners and place in the freezer until set. Keep them stored in the fridge.

White Chocolate Butter Pecan

Ingredients:

- 2 tbsp coconut oil
- ½ c chopped pecans
- 2 tbsp butter
- A pinch of salt
- 2-oz cocoa butter
- A pinch of Stevia
- 2 tbsp erythritol, powdered
- ¼ tsp vanilla

Instructions:

Put the cocoa butter, butter, and coconut oil in a pot and melt them together. Remove from heat. Mix the erythritol into the melted mixture, and then stir in the salt.

Mix in the Stevia, if you want to use it, and then mix in the vanilla. Place three pecans into the bottom of some cupcake molds. Pour the white chocolate mixture over the top of each mold. Freeze immediately.

Once done, remove from the mold and keep in the fridge.

Coconut Candies

Ingredients:

- 1 coconut oil, softened
- Desiccated coconut – for rolling
- 1 tsp vanilla
- 1-2 tbsp sweetener
- 2-4 tbsp cocoa powder, unsweetened
- 2 tbsp almond butter
- ½ tsp sea salt

Instructions:

Place everything in your food processor and mix until smooth. Place a tablespoon drops of the mix on parchment paper. Roll them in the coconut and then place in the fridge. Keep stored in the fridge.

Blackberry Coconut

Ingredients:

- 1 c coconut butter
- 1 c coconut oil
- 1 tbsp lemon juice
- ¼ tsp vanilla powder
- ½ c blackberries, frozen
- ½ tsp Stevia drops

Instructions:

Place the coconut butter, blackberries, and coconut oil in a pot and mix everything together. Allow the coconut mixture to cool a bit. Pour this, and the remaining ingredients in a blender and whir up until smooth.

Lay parchment into a square pan and add in the mixture. Refrigerate until hard. Remove and slice into 16 squares. Keep in the fridge.

Pumpkin Pie Bites

Ingredients:

- ½ c pumpkin puree
- ½ c pecans
- 2-oz coconut butter
- 2 tsp pumpkin pie spice
- ½ c coconut oil
- ¼ c erythritol

Instructions:

Melt the coconut oil and soften the coconut butter. Stir together the pumpkin puree, coconut oil, and coconut butter. Mix in the sweetener and then the pumpkin pie spice.

Pour into candy molds or ice cube tray. Toast the pecans in a dry skillet and the press into the fat bombs. Refrigerate until firm and then remove from the molds. Keep refrigerated.

Maple Almond Fudge

Ingredients:

- ½ c almond butter
- 1 tbsp maple syrup
- ¼ c butter
- 2 tbsp coconut oil

Instructions:

Microwave the almond butter, coconut oil, and butter for 30 seconds intervals until mixed. Mix in the maple syrup. Pour mixture into mini cupcake liners and freeze until set. Remove and store in the fridge.

Pecan Pie

Ingredients:

- 1 c chopped pecans
- 1 tsp vanilla
- 2 tbsp Zen sweetener
- 3 tbsp butter
- 2-oz sugar-free chocolate
- ¼ c heavy cream

Instructions:

Brown the butter in a pot. Mix in the cream once it turns golden. Lower heat to simmer. Stir quickly while adding the sweetener and vanilla. Stir for five minutes until thickened.

Take off the heat and mix in the pecans. Place spoonfuls on parchment paper. Freeze for five minutes.

Melt the chocolate and drizzle it over the clusters. Keep them in the fridge.

Cream Cheese Cloud

Ingredients:

- 8-oz softened cream cheese
- ½ tsp vanilla
- ½ c butter, softened
- ¾ c Splenda

Instructions:

Put everything in a bowl and beat until fluffy. Place spoonfuls on parchment paper and freeze an hour. Keep stored in the fridge.

Cinnamon Butter

Ingredients:

- 450 grams butter
- A pinch of Salt
- ¼ c honey
- 1 ½ tsp vanilla
- 1 tbsp cinnamon

Instructions:

Add the butter, vanilla, cinnamon, and honey to a food processor and mix until it is whipped up. Scrape the sides often.

Spoon into silicone molds or dollop on parchment paper. Freeze until solid and keep stored in the fridge.

Caramel Apple Bites

Ingredients:

- 2 green apples, sliced
- A pinch of sea salt
- 5.4-oz coconut cream
- ½ c coconut butter
- 20 drops English Toffee Stevia
- 2 tbsp coconut oil
- 1 tsp cinnamon

Instructions:

Cook the coconut butter, oil, and apple in a pan until the apples have softened. Stir in the cinnamon and make sure the apples have been coated.

Add everything, including the cooked apples in a blender and mix until smooth. Pour into silicone molds and freeze until hard. Take out of the molds and keep them in the fridge.

Pumpkin Spice

Ingredients:

- ½ c coconut oil
- ¼ c Swerve, confectioner
- ¾ c pumpkin puree
- ¼ tsp sea salt
- 1/3 c golden flax
- ½ tsp nutmeg
- 1 tsp cinnamon

Instructions:

Stir everything together in a bowl and place in the freezer for 30 minutes. Remove and roll the mixture into balls. Keep refrigerated.

Prosciutto and Baked Brie

Ingredients:

- 1 slice prosciutto
- 1/8 tsp pepper
- 1-oz Brie, full-fat
- 6 pecan halves

Instructions:

You need your oven at 350. Take a muffin tin and fold the prosciutto in half and slide in a cup so that it lines it. Chop the Brie up into cubes and place inside the prosciutto.

Add in the pecan pieces. Bake for 12 minutes. The cheese should be melted. Let cool ten minutes and enjoy.

Daily Greens

Ingredients:

- ¼ c cocoa powder
- ½ c coconut oil, room temp
- 1 ½ c shredded coconut, unsweetened
- 2 tbsp greens+ O powder

Instructions:

Mix the coconut and greens together and then mix in the coconut oil. Continue mixing until it begins to hold together. Form this into balls and place on parchment. Roll in extra coconut if you want. Place in the fridge for 15 minutes. Put a container and keep in the fridge.

Strawberry Coconut

Ingredients:

- 1/3 c coconut butter
- 1/3 c + 1 tbsp coconut oil
- 1/3 c strawberries, diced
- ½ tbsp cocoa powder
- 1 tbsp shredded coconut, unsweetened
- 8-10 drops liquid Stevia

Instructions:

Mix the coconut butter, Stevia, 1/3 cup coconut oil, cocoa powder together in a double boiler. Place a couple of spoonfuls of water and the strawberries in a pan and cook until soft. Mash the strawberries up.

Add the strawberries and a tablespoon of coconut oil in a blender with some Stevia and mix until smooth. Put the melted coconut mixture in the bottom of some candy molds and then add a teaspoon of the strawberries on top. Top with a bit more coconut.

Harden in the fridge, and then keep stored in the fridge.

Conclusion

Thank for making it through to the end of Ketogenic Fat Bombs. I hope there were many enjoyable desserts for you. Let's hope it was informative and able to provide you with all of the tools you need to achieve your goals.

The next step is to try out some of the fat bomb recipes to improve your energy and your day.

Remember eat these in moderation, I strongly suggest not cooking any more than 2 batches of these fantastic fat bombs a week per person.

Finally, if you found this book useful in any way, a review on Amazon is always appreciated!

70324143R00064

Made in the USA
San Bernardino, CA
27 February 2018